Presenting the expanded second edition

A Crash Course to Learn the

DEVANAGARI SCRIPT

Used for Sanskrit, Hindi, and Marathi Languages

Setubandh Language Series Volume: 4

Prepared by

Bharat S. Shah, M.D.

Setubandh Publications
New York

A Crash Course to Learn the Devanagari Script
Used for Sanskrit, Hindi, and Marathi Languages
By Bharat S. Shah, M.D.

Price: U.S. $ 6.00

First U.S. Edition 1999 (1000 copies)
Expanded Second U.S. Edition 2013

ISBN-13: 978-1484015117
ISBN-10:   1484015118

For a list of books by Bharat S. Shah, M.D. please see the end pages.

PREFACE
To the second expanded edition

There are several factors that persuaded me to prepare this Crash Course. Children born of Indian parents in America, England, and elsewhere including in India have proved themselves to be experts in Medicine, Law, Business, and in computers. They have mastered computer languages like C++, HTML, and many more, whose names we cannot even pronounce. These languages offer the only way to communicate with the computer. It is a painful irony, that our children talk to computers in the latter's own language, but cannot do the same with their own mother!

Children of all ages, from babies to married professionals, are generally able to understand and speak a few words in their mother tongue. But there is only a rare child who can read and write in his or her own language. Many of them are learning vocal music, folk music, religious prayers, and patriotic songs, and take parts in small one-act plays. In all these, their teachers are forced to transliterate everything in English script, e.g., write the Indian national anthem as *Jana-gana-mana-adhinayak jay he,* so that these children can read it.

There is a two-fold problem here. One, transliteration wastes so much precious and scarce energy. Two, not all of us are equally competent to transliterate Sanskrit writings and render them in the English alphabet. Third, English is not a phonetic language with standard pronunciations. Father Vasudev and son Vasudev (Lord Krushna) both are written in an identical manner in English. In our poetic meters *(Chhand)* difference between a short and a long sound is critical. I have seen our friends from the West Indies, third and fourth generation descendants of Indian parents, struggling with *Jaya Jagadish Hare* at the end of their religious ceremonies. Only if they could read Devanagari or Gujarati characters!

If language opens the door to one's culture and religion, its script opens the door to the language. Indian languages are phonetic, relatively fixed in their structure, necessitating learning their basic consonants and vowels only once - a task not too difficult for the young minds that can easily master Greek, Latin, French, and highly technical computer languages. Learning 30-40 basic characters of alphabet shouldn't be a daunting task for them.

They find Indian scripts unfamiliar, and they cannot be taught in the traditional way in which we all were taught. This Course applies an innovative method of teaching the vowel chain *(Barakhshari)* first, then its use with English consonants, then the new characters, and then finally introducing conjoined consonants, special characters, etc. in a friendly and painless way. I have personally taught this course to several students groups, to find their invariable final comment: "I didn't believe it was *this* easy!"

In large groups of 60-70 students, I found it fun to play a game of Bingo (Housey) while introducing the Indian alphabets. The first student able to write his or her name completely from the letters just introduced is the winner. He receives an applause from all. The game continues to declare more and more winners, and ultimately to cover all letters, by which time everybody is a winner! The course can take 1.5 to 3 hours, not a bad investment to be able to learn to read and write almost anything and everything in one's own language, hithertofore avoided out of unnecessary fear.

This Course teaches only the script, and not the language, or its grammar, syntax, proverbs, etc. It is meant for children of Indian parents, their Indian and foreign spouses, friends, and for students and teachers of languages. It can be adapted to teach other Indian, and possibly non-Indian tongues. I hope this will help to serve their purpose.

When the first edition went to press in 1999, my wife was desperately awaiting a liver transplant, and the first edition did not have a preface. I am happy to report that she has survived to see this second expanded edition. I am highly grateful for the enthusiasm with which the students and other readers have greeted this course, as reflected in some of their comments that appeared on the website of amazon.com and are reproduced on the back cover.

My friend and the owner of the Graphic Arts Unlimited, Nandini Shah had printed the first edition of this crash course and had prepared its artistic cover. Nandini and her husband Rohit had worked with me since the inception of the Gujarati Literary Academy of North America, and have had participated in one-act-plays competitions. Unfortunately, Nandini has not survived long enough to see her painstakingly prepared cover page grace this second edition as well.

Bharat S. Shah, M.D.
New York
June 24, 2013.

TABLE OF CONTENTS

Preface

A Crash Course to Learn
THE DEVANAGARI SCRIPT
For Hindi, Marathi, and Sanskrit Languages

Like many things in life, to read and write in the Devanagari script (that is, Sanskrit, Hindi, or Marathi language) is not as difficult as you may have thought it to be, and admittedly, not as easy as I may have presumed. However, the two of us together can certainly make it work. Even if you do not know a single word in any of these languages, it is no problem. If you do know, that will help.

Goal

Our emphasis will be on "reading," that is, being able to recognize the letters (characters) of the alphabet, numerals and various punctuation marks (a comma, a period, a question mark, etc.) You will begin to write also. When we are done, you should be able to write your own name, those of your family and friends, all characters of the alphabet, numbers like 10524, fractions like ¾, and decimals like 25.765. You will also be able to read and write anything and everything in the Devanagari script, without knowing their meaning, though.

Scope

We will limit ourselves to reading and writing the characters of the alphabet and the numerals. We will not go into the language itself—synonyms, antonyms, grammar, letter writing, proverbs, poetry, vocabulary, etc. This is just to familiarize you with the language and to get you going with confidence. You may request help from someone who knows Devanagari, e.g., your parents, teacher, spouse, a friend, or anyone else who can answer your questions, when you ask. You do not need that individual to sit down with you all the while you are going through this course.

About this course

This is a programmed text, unlike the traditional books. This work makes sure that a concept has been understood, before going to the next one. Now on, please **keep the right margin covered with a card 2x10," leaving the horizontal arrows visible.** Give yourself a pat on the back if you know the answer, and if you do not, I will tell you.

The table of contents is usually not a part of a programmed text. However, I have included one for easily finding something that you may need to refer to. Do not try to memorize anything. Also, do not write down pronunciations in English, which is not a phonetic language and will make your task more difficult.

I have tried my best to guide you with writing and pronouncing the Devanagari characters. However, those can only be approximations. The scope of this work limits me from doing more. I have put a video *(Devanagari Characters: How to Write and pronounced Them)* on the YouTube *http://www.youtube.com/watch?v=yN3f8Hur8X4.*

Vowels and Vowel Symbols:

Let us begin with the word 'America'. Since we would prefer to have only one letter represent only one sound, and because 'C' conveys 'S' sound (Nice), and also a 'K' sound (Cut, Car), let us replace 'C' with 'K', thus: Amerika. In this word, there are two 'a's, the first, and the last letters, and both are pronounced differently. We will underline the second (last) 'a', thus: Amerik<u>a</u>.

'A' sound as in 'alone', 'American Indian'
'<u>A</u>' sound as in 'c<u>a</u>r', 'F<u>a</u>r'

In Devanagari, instead of writing out the whole vowels (A, E, I, O, U) after each consonant, we use their symbols. The symbol for '<u>a</u>' is a vertical line like this: T. It follows the letter: ∎T (where the box ∎ is any letter of the alphabet).

☞ Note that the horizontal line at the top of all letters is characteristic of the Devanagari script.

Amerik<u>a</u>	becomes	→	A me ri kT
C<u>a</u>r	becomes	→	KT r
B<u>a</u>r	becomes	→	BT r

Similarly, the vowel symbol for 'I' (as in 'India') is fʼ∎ and it goes before the letter. The 'ri' in 'Amerika' will become fʼr :

Amerika	becomes	→	A me fʼr kT
Mita	becomes	→	fʼM tT
Gira	becomes	→	fʼG rT

We can replace 'e' with an inverted check mark over the letter (■`), to change 'me' in America into m` and

Ame f̂rkⲦ	becomes	→	A m̀ f̂rkⲦ
Patel	becomes	→	Pa t l̀

If you put a slightly modified f̂■ behind a letter thus ■ⲦÎ, then you get 'ee' sound:

Geeta	→	Gî tⲦ
Meet	→	Mî t

Just as f̂■ and ■Î for 'I' and 'EE' go before and after a letter, the symbols for 'U' and 'OO' both go under it. The symbol for 'U' is ▮ and for 'OO' is ▮. For example:

Put	→	P̦ t
Roof	→	R̦ f
Booth	→	R̦ th
Bush	→	B̦ sh

And to refresh your memory, write these:

Bath	→	BⲦ th
Bit	→	f̂B t
Beet	→	Bî t

In English, there are five basic vowels, viz. A, E, I, O, U. Of these, we did not cover 'O' yet. For 'O' we do not need any new symbol, but will combine two symbols we already know: ∎ⓣ and ∎.

Hold	→	Hⓣ ld
Pole	→	Pⓣ le
Polo	→	Pⓣ Lⓣ

There are some less frequently used combinations. Instead of one inverted check mark, we can use two:

∎   and   ∎ⓣ   instead of   ∎   and   ∎ⓣ
'Ai'   and   'Au'   instead of   'E'   and   'O'

Jain	J n	(Does not rhyme with PAIN).
Vaishnav	V shna v	
Kailas	K la s	
Gautama	Gⓣ ta ma	
Aurangzeb	Aⓣ ran g z b	(The last Moghul emperor)

Note that 'Au' is not pronounced as in 'Automobile.' It is 'A' (the first 'A' in 'America') and 'U' (as in 'Put') said in rapid sequence. 'Ai' is 'A' and 'I' (as in 'India') said in rapid sequence.

☞ It is better to ask someone to show you how to pronounce 'Ai' and 'Au,' because in English these sound are not used.

A dot on the top of a letter, ∎ indicates the nasal 'UM' or 'UN' sound. Now, see these words:

Aurangzeb	A̍ rǵz̀b
Hunt	H ṫ
Hunch	H ċh
Apartment	A p̄ rt m̀ t
Dentist	D̀ t̂ st
Lint	L̂ t

Try to read the following:

Ȧ K L   →   (Uncle)

Ā T̂   →   (Auntee)

A̤ M̄   →   (Uma)

Ā G L   →   (Eagle)

The next and the last symbol, which is extremely commonly used in Sanskrit, looks like a colon (:) and is put after a letter ■: to indicate breathing out completely saying 'oh' or 'ah,' etc.

P:	P-H		P̄:	Pa-Ha
P̤:	Pu-Hu		P̂:	Po-Ho

That concludes our vowel symbols. Let me list them for you:

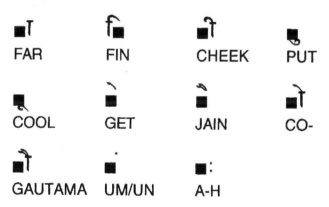

■̄	f■	■̂	■̤
FAR	FIN	CHEEK	PUT
■̤	■̀	■̇	■̄
COOL	GET	JAIN	CO-
■̂	■	■:	
GAUTAMA	UM/UN	A-H	

The last two symbols actually do not represent any vowels, but they are tagged on after other vowel symbols.

Let me point out to you again that these symbols save a lot of time and trouble. Instead of writing out the vowels A, I, EE, U, OO, E, AI, O, AU after each and every consonant, we just write these symbols. Moreover, a simple little dot on top of a letter replaces so many 'M' and 'N's. The best is yet to come!

Vowel With No Symbol:

Read these words (never mind their meaning for now):

Bharat	Raman	Saral
Manan	Nayan	Charan
Dhaval	Gaman	

We used 43 characters to write these words (I counted them for you) in English, of which there are 27 consonants, and 16 vowels. 16 out of 43 is 37%. In Devanagari, we drop all such 'A' sounds altogether. That is a nearly 40% saving in labor right there. We use no symbol for this 'A' sound. No symbol means A, as the first 'A' in 'America'.

☞ In Devanagari, no symbol is used to represent "A" (the first "A" in America)

Take the words listed above. In Devanagari, we write all these words as shown below (without the spaces between the letters):

BH R T	R M N	S R L
M N N	N Y N	CH R N
DH V L	G M N	

So, now you know how to write in Devanagari, using the English alphabet and Devanagari vowel symbols with any letter.

Now, let us try these with a consonant like "M" to indicate the vowel sounds

M Mा fM Mी M M
M̀ M̂ Mी Mी M M:

It works the same way with any other consonant like P, Z, G, T, D, etc. With consonants (i.e., letters other than A, E, I, O, U) we use symbols for vowels. These symbols are never used alone, by themselves, without a consonant.

☞ The vowel symbols are never used without a consonant.

Creating MoreVowels By Using Symbols:

For using the vowels themselves as letters, we use the forms of 'A'. The basic vowel 'A' (the first...) is written thus: अ.

Try to write the letter अ with vowel symbols:

→ अ आ इ ई
अु अू ए ऐ
ओ औ अं अ:

However, for convenience (certainly not yours), a few of the vowels are written in a different way, e.g.,

अि	is written as	इ
अी	"	ई
अु	"	उ
अू	"	ऊ
अे	"	ए
अै	"	ऐ

The last two above can be very confusing. Look at these carefully. ए has no inverted check mark on top, unlike in अे. ऐ has only one, instead of the two we see in अै. The vowel series, therefore, looks like this:

Look at the chain of twelve symbols above. This chain is called BARAKSHARI or BARAKHADI (literally, 'a chain of twelve letters'), pronounced as Bॊ Rॊ KH Dॊ .

It is very important to understand when to use the symbols, and when to use the various forms of letter अ as shown above. Let us see a few examples.

Write these in Devanagari or English script (mixed):

America	→	अ MĪRKĪ
India	→	ई िDYī
Indiana	→	ई िDYīNī
England	→	ई॔ GL D
Overpass	→	ओVRPīS
Israel	→	ईZRईL
Andy	→	ए॔ Dी
Airavat (Divine elephant with seven tusks)	→	ऐRीVT
Arab	→	आRB

As you can see, the same symbols are used to modify the consonants, and also to modify the basic vowel अ to generate other vowels. In other words, various forms of consonants and various vowels are generated by using the same symbols, in the same manner.

☞ Symbols are used with consonants, or with the basic vowel अ in the same manner.

Meet the Devanagari Alphabet:

Believe it or not, you are ready to write in Devanagari now, using the Devanagari alphabet. You may or may not know any Sanskrit words. First, write your own name, those of your family members, your friends, or significant others, using vowel symbols and English consonants.

Write:

Your name	BHARAT	→
Father's name	SHANTILAL	→
Mother's name	KANTABEN	→
Any name	USHA	→

Now, write those names breaking them up into their syllables like this:

BHA RA T	→
SHAN TI LA L	→
KAN TA BE N	→
U SHA	→

Now write them using the symbols, and Devanagari letters that you may know:

BH R T	→
SHĨTLĨL	→
KĨTĨBN	→
ƆSHĨ	→

Now there are two options:

1.   If it is possible, ask your parents or someone else familiar with Sanskrit, to show you how to write only the letters of your name in Devanagari. Just the letters, not the whole name. Say, your name is KOKILA (a girl's name), then ask them to show you K and L only. Then you fill in the symbols for O, I and A.

2.   If there is no such easily accessible help, I have provided on the next page a list of Devanagari equivalents of English alphabet. You may look up and find the letters needed to write all the names on your list.

DEVANAGARI EQUIVALENTS OF ENGLISH CHARACTERS

A	अ, आ, ■, ■ा						
B	ब		Bh	भ			
C	स	(Cycle)	Ch	च		Chh	छ
	क	(Cycle)					
D	द, ड		Dh	ध, ढ			
E	■े, ए		EE	■ी, ई, अी			
F/Ph	फ		G	ज	(George, "Jyo")	Jh	झ
				ग	(God)	Gh	घ
H	ह						
I	■ि, अि, इ		EE	■ी, अी, ई			
J	ज		Jh/z	झ			
K	क		Kh	ख			
L	ल		L/R	ळ			
M	म, ■ं		N	न, ण, ■ं			
O	■ो, ओ		OO	■ू, ऊ, अू			
P	प		Ph/F	फ		Qu	क्व
R	र		R/L	ळ			
S	स		SH	श, ष			
T	त	(Et tu!)	Th	थ	(Theme, Theory)		
				ध	(The, Then)		
	ट	(Brute?)		ठ	('Total' said as 'Thothal')		
U	■ु, उ, अु		OO	■ू, ऊ, अू			
V/W	व		X(KS)	क्ष	(KSH)		
Y	य		Z/Jh	झ			

Feel free to refer to this list as you go along. You will remember these by practice. I will write a few names here, and you may want to write a few more. Since I don't know your name, let us begin with mine. My name is BHARAT. We will write it like this: Bh R T.

There are several sounds like Bh, Ph, Gh, Dh, Th, etc. that are written in English as two letters, B and h, and so on. In Devanagari, they are indeed represented by only one letter. Let us also treat them as one letter.

Bh R T	is	Bharat
Dh Nी	is	Dhani (a girl's name)
Ghी Rी	is	Ghari (a sweet)
Aी Dhी R	is	Adhar (a support)
िPh Lे Sे Phी	is	Philosophy

Soon, I will stop writing the English pronunciations. You can check the list to find that—

Bh	is written as	भ	
R	"	र	
T	"	त	(also as ट. That's why it is better to ask).

So, we write my name as भरत. We did not need any vowel symbols here. But suppose we want to write BHARATI, a girl's name. Then we need to use the vowel symbols:

BHARATI	→	Bhा R ती	→	भारती
USHA	→	अ Shा	→	अुषा (उषा)
UMA	→	अ Mा	→	अुमा (उमा)
NIKHIL	→	िN िKh L	→	निखिल
MANISHA	→	M Nी Shा	→	मनीषा
PIYUSH	→	िP Y Sh	→	पियूष

As for the consonants, you already know ten of them, viz. BH, R, T, M, N, SH, KH, L, Y, and P written as भ, र, त, म, न, ष, ख, ल, य and प respectively, in Devanagari. You may be able to use them in writing the names from your list, or you may need more letters. Even if you do only one or two names every day, you will know the entire Devanagari alphabet (all 36 letters) pretty soon.

☞ Note the horizontal line at the top of all consonants and vowels, and of the vowel symbols touching the top line: म, न, ष, अ, ई, ◼ा, ि◼ and ◼ी.

The Rest of the Alphabet:

Learn the rest of the alphabet slowly, at your own pace. Since you may have a very limited vocabulary in Sanskrit, if any at all, at first you may practice writing English words in Devanagari script.

Devanagari is a phonetic alphabet, unlike English. Therefore, you can write any English word in Devanagari. You never have to guess its pronunciation. One piece of advice.

☞   Follow the sound, not the spelling!

Uncle	is	अंकल,	not	अुंकल
			or	उंकल

But	„	बट,	not	बुट
Kid	„	किड	„	कईड
The	„	ध or धी		

Before we go further, try to write a few words that you already know:

America	→	अमेरिका
Russia	→	रशिया
London	→	लंडन
Devanagari	→	देवनागरी
Ganesh (Lord Ganesh)	→	गणेश
Total	→	टोटल
Ramesh (a boy's name)	→	रमेश

Using the letters you already know, you may try to write a few English words. Try the following:

Paris	→	You try it, please!
Rio De Janero	→	
Natavarlal	→	
Yashavant	→	
Kamini	→	O.K. Read on.

You should have no trouble reading the following words:

नटवरलाल	→	See below.
यशवंत	→	
पेरिस	→	
रीयो डी जानेरो, रीयो डी हेनेरो	→	
कामिनी	→	These are the same words that I asked you to write in the previous paragraph! I will show you soon, how to write "Paragraph".

Let us write a few more words:

Jagat (World)	→	जगत
Jel (a jail), to gel	→	जेल
Chair	→	चेर
Bazaar (Market place)	→	बाझार
Mahesh	→	महेश
Hawaii	→	हवाई

Write:

Ghar	(a house)	→	घर
Vagh	(a tiger)	→	वाघ
Bagh	(a tiger)	→	बाघ
Bag	(rhymes with <u>B</u>aptism. A garden)	→	बाग

We are almost done. You probably thought we would never finish.

Let us write

Thought	→	थोट
Thick	→	थिक
Think	→	थिंक

The next letter ठ is also 'Th', but not as in 'Think', or in 'The'. When you say 'Total' very harshly, like 'Thothal', you are close. Similarly, ढ is also 'Dh', but not like in 'The'. It sounds like a harshly said 'Damn', i.e. 'Dhem'. It is a sound that is unique to Sanskrit. To approximate it, retroflex your tongue, don't let it touch the back of your teeth, and say ड (D) harshly, while breathing out.

ढाका	Dhaka	(Capital of Bangladesh)
ढेल	Dhel	(a pea-hen)
ढोल	Dhol	(a drum)

Just a few more letters to go. फ is very easy. It is 'F' or 'Ph'. We Indians do not discriminate between the two. The same for 'V' and 'W' as well.

☞   In Devanagari, F and PH, as well as V and W, are treated as the same.

Try to write:

Philosophy   → फिलोसोफी

Joseph   → जोसेफ

Fine   → फाईन

Hala (a plow)   → हळ

In 'Hala' above, both 'a's are अ, and not आ. The letter ळ has a peculiar pronunciation. It is between 'R' and 'L', or र and ल. Try to say 'R' and then 'L'. Note where the tongue touches the palate. Now move the tongue to a position between the two, and say ळ. If you cannot, you can say 'ल' for now. No word begins with ळ. It is rarely used.

There are two more letters with which no words begin. Unlike ळ, they are not even generally written. They are ङ and ञ ('Ung' and 'Yn'). Both are nasal sounds. They are ghost letters. Let us see how to write "Ghost".

Consonants Joined Together
(For better or for worse)!

Sometimes two or more letters (consonants) are joined together without a vowel ('conjoined consonants'), as in GHO<u>ST</u>, RI<u>SK</u>, DUM<u>PST</u>ER, BHA<u>SK</u>AR, <u>SM</u>ITA in which the underlined consonants are joined together without a vowel. If your list contains any names like that, for the time being you can add अ and break up the conjoined ones as follows:

SMITA → S िMिTा → समिता
(Sa MI TA)

BHASKAR → BHि S K R → भासकर
(BHA SA KA R)

MRIDULA → M Rी दु Lा → मरीदुला
(MA RI DU LA)

Now, you know a few more letters, viz. स, क, र, and द for 'S', 'K', 'R', and 'D' respectively. But SA MI TA is not Smita, and BHA SA KA R is not Bhaskar.

We want to join स + म, स + क, म + र. Both these letters, स and म, contain a vertical line to your right (स is र + ा). We simply drop that line, and then join the remaining with the consonant that follows it.

स मि ता → र् मिता → स्मिता
(स्म is one letter)

भा स क र → भास् कर → भास्कर

व त स ला → वत् सला → वत्सला

Historically, there was a vowel written as ऋ and is now used to convey 'RI' sound (no ी to follow. Not ऋी, but ऋ), and its remnants show up very commonly as ◼ or ◼ to indicate the half 'R' sound.

पा र व ती → पा◼वती → पार्वती (Parvati)

श र ट → श◼ट → शर्ट (a shirt)

क रु ष ण → क◼ष ण → कृष्ण,

not कृष्णा
(Lord Krishna)

म री दु ला → म◼दुला → मृदुला (Mridula)
(a girl's name)

☞ Note that ◼ is part of a vowel. It is used only with consonants, and not with other vowels. There is no "R" sound in ई (ई).

Add to your list the vowel (ऋ), and consonants क, ण, श, व, and ट. Are you able to write all, or any, of the names on your list? Maybe, you need a few more letters.

Write all the vowels and their symbols:

अ	आ	इ	ई
◼	◼ा	ि◼	◼ी

उ	ऊ	ए	ऐ
◼	◼	◼	◼

ओ	औ	अं	अः
◼ो	◼ौ	◼ं	◼ः

| ऋ (Ri) | | ◼ | ◼ |

The letters like क, ट, र, etc. have no vertical lines built into their right end. So, they are physically attached to the next consonants, if a conjoined consonant is needed.

क त (K T)	क्त (KT) (No vertical line)	
but, त स (T S)	त्स (TS) (Vertical line dropped)	
स ट (S T)	स्ट (ST) (Vertical line dropped)	
and त क (T K)	त्क (TK) (Vertical line dropped)	

You should be able to write these:

Delhi	→	दिल्ही
Saraswati (goddess of learning)	→	सरस्वती
Ghost	→	घोस्ट
Moscow	→	मोस्को
Fortunate	→	फोर्च्युनेट

Special Characters:

Over hundreds of years, several pairs of conjoined consonants have undergone changes because of frequent writings and inevitable evolution. Some of them have evolved into special characters, in which the original individual members may not be easily recognizable. A conjoined pair is treated as one letter.

In the following special characters, the first letter is halved, that is, its vowel is removed.

Try to identify the consonants that are joined:

पत्र	(Patr)	A letter	→	त	+	र
प्रेम	(Prem)	Love	→	प	+	र
श्री.	(Shri)	Mr.	→	श	+	र
श्रीमती	(Shrimati)	Mrs.				
ट्राम	(Tram)	Tram	→	ट	+	र
पार्ट	(Part)	Part, and so on.				
कृष्ण	(Krishn)	Lord Krishna				
हृदय	(Hriday)	Heart	→	ह	+	◖
तृप्ति	(Tripti)	Satisfaction				
पद्म	(Padm)	Lotus	→	द	+	म
सह्य	(Sahy)	Bearable	→	ह	+	य

Write the following:

Sentence	→ सेन्टेन्स
Evaluation	→ इवेल्युएशन
Paragraph	→ पेरेग्राफ
Savitri (a mythological woman's name)	→ सावित्री

If any of the names in your list contain such characters, learn to write them as such. That's life! You and I cannot stop evolution. Eventually you will learn them, too. They are fun, and kind of cute.

A Special Way of Writing:

Many of the special characters shown above came about thanks to an old tradition of writing half letters literally on the top of the complete letter that follows them. Depending upon the typeface (fonts) used in printing, these special characters may or may not be easy to identify.

Whenever any such letter is not clear enough, I have tried to avoid using it in this book. However, you should be able to recognize them.

Half	ह	+	ऋ	=	हृ
	ह		म		ह्म
	ह		न		ह्
	ह		य		ह्य

→ (Gujarati font, for demonstration only. The Devanagari character would have a horizontal line at the top)

द	द	द्द
द	व	द्व
द	ऋ	द्
द	र	द्र
द	ध	द्ध
द	म	द्म

न	न	न, न्
च	च	च्
ट	ट	ट्
ळ	ळ	ळ्

22

श　　च　　श्र

श　　व　　श्व　　　→　(As above)

Special Letters:

There are two more letters of the alphabet, that are actually not basic, but are in fact, conjoined consonants, and have evolved as special characters. The first one represents the "KSH" sound, as the last "X" in "Xerox".

अ क श त → अव् श त → अक्षत

(क्ष is क् + श)

The last letter to know has much to do with knowledge. It is said as 'Gna' or as 'Gnya' wherein the 'a's are अ.

ज्ञान	Gnan, Gnyan	(Knowledge)
आज्ञा	Aagna, Agnya	(an order)
द्राक्ष	Draksh	(Grapes)

☞　These two letters are in fact, conjoined consonants, and have evolved as special charatcters.

☞　Note that in pronouncing the conjoined consonants, the accent is on the letter that precedes both of them.

Punctuation Marks:

In addition to consonants and vowels, our writing contains punctuation marks. Fortunately at present, they are used exactly the same way in Devanagari, as they are in English. The same comma (,), quotes (' ') or (" "), question mark (?), exclamation mark (!), and so on, are used, not to leave out the semi colon (;), and colon (:).

☞ In modern Sanskrit, punctuation marks are used the same way as in English, except the period.

The comma and the quotes are not used in classical Sanskrit. Modernized Sanskrit writings do contain all the modern punctuation marks. There is some slight difference though. The period (.) at the end of a sentence, is represented in Devanagari as a vertical line, without any horizontal line at the top, thus: ।.

This is a boy.   This is a boy ।

His name is Ashok.   His name is Ashok ।

Sometimes you may see two such lines, especially in a stanza of a poem.

टवीन्कल टवीन्कल लिटल स्टार

हाउ आई वन्डर वोट यु आर   ।

अप अेबोव ध वर्ल्ड सो हाय

लाइक अ डायमन्ड इन ध स्काय ॥

Were you able to read the above, word by word?

→ It is "Twinkle, twinkle, little star!"

Numerals, Fractions, and Decimals:

Words are made of one (a, I) or more letters of the alphabet. Numbers are made of one (1-0) or more numerals. Numerals are used in the same way as in English.

१	२	३	४	५
1	2	3	4	5

६	७	८	९	०
6	7	8	9	0

As you can see, the numeral 0 is identical, and 1, 2, and 3 are similar in both languages. The rest are easy to learn. Also remember, there is no horizontal line at the top of any numeral, or of punctuation marks.

☞ The numerals are used in the same way as in English. There is no horizontal line at the top of any numeral or of punctuation marks.

☞ All numbers, fractions and decimals are written the same way as in English. Mathematical symbols like plus (+), minus (-), times (x), division (÷), and square root (√) are used in the same way as in English.

$$२ \times ४ = ८$$
$$१५ + २० = ३५$$
$$१५^२ = २२५$$
$$\sqrt{२२५} = १५$$

More About the Alphabet
A Review and Practice

This chapter should be sheer fun, provided you have been following the program instructions properly. If not, it may be a waste of time to go ahead. By now you should be able to read and write almost anything and everything that is written in the Devanagari script.

In the beginning of the previous chapter I threw the alphabet at you. Now I will show you slowly, how various letters are written. Also, I will help by showing you how to pronounce the sounds conveyed by certain letters properly.

I will give you a few hints to quickly recognize various characters, and will tell you many interesting tidbits.

In this chapter you will get more practice, making you feel more at home with the Devanagari script, and soon you will be prepared to take a real plunge in the Sanskrit language itself.

Write the numeral that is common between English and Devanagari.

→ ० (Zero)

Let us take another one. Take the letter "R", then split it in the middle vertically, I + २. The part on your right, "२" is Devanagari numeral २ (two).

Write the numeral two, in Devanagari.

→ २

The same numeral २, with a line at the top becomes the Devanagari equivalent of the letter "R", thus:

→ र

Write two Devanagari numerals, and one letter:

→ ०, २, र

What is the difference between the numeral two, and the letter "R" in Devanagari?

→ The letter has a line at the top, while the numeral does not.
२ (two), र (R).

The letter र is not called (AR) as in P<u>ar</u>k, but is called "r" as in Fu<u>r</u>. No ef (F), or ech (H), but simply "F" as in blu<u>ff</u>, or "H" as in <u>H</u>ut.

☞ Devanagari letters are named after the sounds they convey.

☞ In Devanagari, "0" (Zero) does not double as the letter "O" (Operator).

Which Devanagari numeral doubles as a letter?

→ २

Which letter does it become?

→ र

What sound does that letter convey?

→ R

Can you write "twenty" in Devanagari?

→ २० (Not र०)

Two hundred?

→ २०० (Not र००)

You should not be surprised that 2, 20, 200, etc. are written in the same way in both languages. Why not ?

→ The zero was invented in India for this purpose. Then it went to the Western world.

Let us take another letter. You do recognize the "S" as in Sam, Sleep, etc. We can put it to sleep, and cut it in the middle with a vertical line, like this: क. Note the line at the top. This letter is equivalent of "K", or of "C" as in <u>C</u>ut, Do<u>c</u>, Lo<u>c</u>k, etc.

How do you pronounce क ?

> → "K" sound as in <u>K</u>ite, <u>C</u>ut, Do<u>c</u>

It does look like two "C"s with a cut in the middle, doesn't it?

With a slight modification of क, we get another letter, which is फ. It is pronounced as "PH" or "F". There is no distinction between these two sounds in Devanagari.

How would you say फ ?

> → "F" as in Cu<u>ff</u>, or <u>f</u>ur.

This letter फ does remind me of an "F" which has fallen over on its back, to our left.

Write in Devanagari:

Cuff	→	कफ
Rough	→	रफ
Fur	→	फर
Of	→	ओफ.

> ० (zero) does not double as a letter. "०फ" is incorrect.

Read:

कर	→	K.R
रक	→	R.K
०	→	Zero. It is called "Shoonya". You do not have to remember that.

We did look at the letter "S". In Devanagari, there is a letter which is written in the same way, like this: ड. This conveys the "D" sound, as in Dog, Doll, etc. When you write "d", you may wonder whether it is written as "d" or as "b". The letter ड is for a dilemma, and it apparently combines parts of "d" and "b" to remind us how to write it! Although it may look different in print, it is written like the letter "S", thus: ड.

Write in Devanagari:

Duck	→	डक
Two Duck(s)	→	२ डक
No Duck	→	० डक

The letter ड with a dot in the upper notch, like this: ङ is another letter, one with a nasal sound, like "ong/ung" as in T<u>ong</u>ue. This is an interesting letter, in that no word begins with it. In the modern descendants of Sanskrit, ङ is never actually written. In Sanskrit it is written, but it is often replaced with a dot on top of the previous letter.

Say these:

ड	→	D
ङ	→	Ung/Ong
Dunk	→	डंक
Fund	→	फंड
(Ge)rund	→	(Ge)रंड

In Fund and Gerund, the dot represents "N", whereas in "Dunk", it represents ङ. Say "Dunk" and "Fund" out loud a couple of times to see the difference in the nasal sounds.

Which English letters convey the nasal sounds?

→ M and N.

These also occur in Sanskrit. Later, I will show you how to write these. So, there are N and M, plus there is ङ, that makes three. There are two more, for a total of five letters with nasal sounds.

Don't let that bother you. All five, each one, when used to represent a nasal twang, can be represented by the dot on the top of the previous letter. Of the five, only *M* and *N* may occur at the beginning of a word, while ङ and the other two nasal letters do not.

Use English letters (Devanagari ones, if you know them) and the dot to write the following:

Pump	→	ṖP	पंप
Bunk	→	Ḃक	बंक
Bump	→	ḂP	बंप
Bunt	→	ḂT	बंट

31

Write "Tongue" (as before) →   तंग   टंग

You can easily write Pump using Devanagari letters also. You write "P" backwards, like this: "q", and then open it up, and put a line at the top, as always: प. This is "P" as in <u>P</u>um<u>p</u> .

Write:

Pump	→	पंप
Punk (mud)	→	पंक
Kump (a shiver)	→	कंप
Puff	→	पफ

Note how similar प (P) and फ (Ph) are.

Couple	→	कपल
Dump	→	डंप

The letter प can be modified to make a numeral: ५, which resembles a calligraphic lower case "y". This is the numeral 5. Its relation to the letter प is a bit more obvious in Devanagari, wherein the numeral ५ (5) is called "Punch" as in Hawaiian Punch. "Punch" means "Five".

Write:

Punch	→	पंच
Three Devanagari numerals	→	०, २, ५
Write Six Devanagari letters	→	र प क फ ड ङ

By now you really understand the concept of representing the nasal sounds with a symbol (■̇) rather than a whole letter. In English, you have to write Pump, Tongue, etc, while in Devanagari a mere dot (■) will do, where ■ is any letter of the alphabet.

There are twelve such symbols to simplify our life. The dot is only one of them. Most of the remaining symbols stand for vowels.

Write English vowels: → A, E, I, O, U.

Write a few combinations of these vowels to produce different sounds. → AU, EE, OO, etc.

Write the symbols for these. → ■ी, ■ी, ■ॢ.

Writing The Devanagari Letters:

In English, all capital letters neatly fit between two horizontal lines: ADGTBNHJMOVCXS.

The lower case letters may fit between the two lines, or they may project above and/or below the lines: acsxz bdkl pquj.

Some do this only part way: **ABCD tji.**

However, all the letters can be accomodated in three equal segments, created by drawing four lines:

ABCD mncszx tfji pqbdy. A b q a

In the above, **m n c s z x** occupy the middle segment. Let us compare this with Devanagari.

As you know, there are no capital and lower case letters in Devanagari. However, we have various vowel symbols that extend above and below the main letters. However, the proportion of various letters allotted to these spaces is slightly different.

The projections above and below the lines are only half the height of the main letters. That is, if we divide the writing space in four equal parts (not three), then the main body of the letter occupies the middle two parts, leaving one part above, and one below. Note the proportions:

क प र जा ला मि शी डे टै यु सू इं

You may want to use a blank sheet of musical scores to write Devanagari letters. Parts of a few letters themselves also extend above and/or below the lines:

क ख   ह क्ष भ ञ झ

In the above, the first two letters are confined to their own space. The remaining ones extend either in front of the top line, e.g., क्ष, भ or below the base line, e.g., ह, क्ष, ञ, झ, or both, e.g., क्ष.

Similar But Not the Same:

As you can see from the table of Devanagari and English letters, there are several groups of similar letters. See त, न, म, and भ.

As you know, न and म are nasal. You may also remember that they can be represented by a dot over the previous letter, as in the following:

पंकज

डंक

सेइंट   (a saint)

सेंट   (a scent)

One clarification is in order. They are not always replaced by dot. For example:

मनीषा

निखिल

अमेरिका

मेडीसीन

In these, म and न are used as such, with a vowel attached to them. It is only when we need the half or incomplete (without a vowel) म or न sound, that is, when we need ᵐ or ⁿ, then and only then we can replace them with a dot.

The न sound is similar to "N", and is quite familiar to you. It is a dental sound. You can hold your tongue between your teeth and say it. This is the location as well, when you say थ as in थीम (theme).

Now say "Tom", then keep saying "T". Now, try to say न from the same location as ट. Or while saying न..न..न..न..न repeatedly, keep sliding the tongue upward and backward. When the न sound changes, let it change, and repeat that a few times. That is ण, another nasal character, used just like म and न. ण is used very commonly. However no word begins with it.

The last nasal letter conveys the "yn" sound, and it is written as ञ. No word begins with that either.

List the letters with which no word begins: → ण, ञ, ङ, ळ

Which of these letters are practically never written at all?

→ ञ, ङ

What sounds do they represent?

→ "yn", and "ung"

Let us write a few words with the ण sound:

माणेक   A precious stone

पारसमणी   A mythical stone, which converts everything it touches, into gold. "Midas" stone.

पाणी   Water

पाणिनी   The first one to formally write the grammar of Sanskrit.

Today there are many who would rather die than bother to study Sanskrit grammar. It is said that the great grammarian Panini actually gave up his life for it.

Once, while he was engrossed in teaching the Sanskrit grammar to his disciples on the bank of a river, suddenly a tiger appeared there. Disciples screamed, व्याघ्रः ! व्याघ्रः ! ("Tiger! Tiger!"). Panini simply gave them the etymology of the word saying, विशिष्ठा जिघ्रा यस्य सः व्याघ्रः । ("One who has a keen sense of smell, is called a Tiger"!) Disciples, less interested in the grammar, ran away. Tiger did what tigers do. Such was Panini's devotion.

Write:

Chakrap<u>a</u>ni	→	चक्रपाणी (क्र=क् + र)

(one who has a wheel in his hand. Lord Vishnu)

Padmini	→	पद्मिनी (द् + म)
Patang	→	पतंग A kite, a moth

Conservation of Energy and Resources:

Let us go back to the word राम. The way it is written in English, RAMA, it can be pronounced in several ways.

Write in Devanagari, how RAMA can be pronounced:

→ राम, रामा

रमा रम

If we pronounce "A" as in Pat, a boy, man, etc. then there are many more ways it can be written.

In Devanagari, it can be said in only one way, राम.

Now you may appreciate, why it is a waste of time and energy to transliterate Sanskrit into English.

What is "Transliteration"? → To write something from one language in the script of another one. For example: राम RAMA.

How does it differ from translation? → Translation gives the precise meaning using words and script from the new language.

Give some examples of translation and transliteration from this book or from elsewhere:

पंक → Punk (Transliteration).

→ Mud (Translation).

मन → Mana (Transliteration),

→ Mind (Translation)

Sanskrit and its daughters are phonetic languages, i.e., you read exactly the way it is written. Pronunciation does not have to be guessed. English words like Busy, Wonder, Lieutenant, etc. would be impossible for an outsider to pronounce correctly the first time.

Therefore, it is far more reasonable and efficient for one to learn the Devanagari alphabet than expect the entire Sanskrit literature to be transliterated into English. There are many advantages of learning the Devanagari alphabet.

I will not ask you to enumerate the advantages of learning the Devanagari script. One obvious advantage is, you may claim your position as an in-sider, rather than remaining a stranger.

By now, you have a basic concept of how the Devanagari script works, and how it differs from English.

Which one or more of the following would you consider as being helpful to you?

❑ Sanskrit is a phonetic language. So you read it exactly as it is written.
❑ Instead of writing out entire vowels, you write only their symbols.

❑ Sanskrit being a member of the Indo-European family of languages, it shares some words and characteristics with English.
❑ Sanskrit numerals are used in the same way as the English (Arabic) ones are.

Add any more advantages that you can think of:

→ 1.
2.
3.
4.
5.

Together or Apart?

In this chapter, we will go over some important and peculiar points of the Devanagari letters. It is easy to confuse RV (रव) and KH (ख). You can tell them apart by looking at the closeness of र and व in ख. The top line may have a small gap between र and व, in रव. When you know the words, the context may help differentiate them.

☞ Do not confuse the following similar looking characters:

रव	र व
ख	KH
श्व	श + व,
स्त्र	स + त्र (व or त + र)
स्र	स + र

Bite Your Tongue!

Another trouble spot for Westerners is in the following letters. In English, both rows are written as follows:

T   Th   D   Dh   N

ट   ठ   ड   ढ   ण
त   थ   द   ध   न

Each row of Devanagari letters above belongs to a distinct class. Its member letters are pronounced while the tongue is touching the same part of the mouth. The lowest row sounds are dental. You can literally hold the tongue between your teeth and say these letters. We did that when we talked about न.

You probably have no trouble saying न as in Nut, थ as in Theme, and ध as in There. Now, try to say the त and द while holding your tongue between your teeth.

The same is the case with the upper Devanagari row. For saying ठ, ढ, and ण, Try to say थ, ध, and न respectively, but without letting your tongue anywhere near your teeth. Say these by retroflexing the tongue, that is curling it up, and touching the palate with its tip.

All this is supposed to be fun. It may not make you laugh, but it should be of interest. I am not asking you to memorize anything. There is one quirk that deserves to be mentioned.

In the top Devanagari row, ठ and ढ both start out (in writing) as ट. Then, in ठ you have a complete loop, while in ढ there is a spiral, ending in a small loop.

Now for some genuine fun. ढ is the 14th letter of the alphabet. In my mother tongue Gujarati, a daughter of Sanskrit, there is a put-down for a stupid person or a moron, which goes like this: "(s)he is like a ढ", or "is the 14th letter of the alphabet!"

Why blame the poor ढ? Because the language has undergone profound changes from the parent languages of Sanskrit (Brahmi, etc.), through its daughter languages like Gujarati. While all other letters have been transformed severely, only ढ has managed to remain totally unaffected! I think it deserves to be honored.

Practice, Practice, Practice!

Your ballpoint pen is probably drying out. Try to write the following words entirely in the Devanagari script:

Car	→	कार
Food	→	फूड
Done	→	डन
Mud	→	मड
Uncle	→	अंकल, अन्कल
Asia	→	एशिया
Austria	→	ओस्ट्रिया

Consulate	→	कोन्स्युलेट
Abort	→	एबोर्ट, अेबोर्ट
Hospital	→	होस्पिटल

One Less Sign to Worry About:

I hope you will forgive my regional pride, if I say that Sanskrit is much older than English, and therefore, it has no symbols to accomodate the broad "O" and broad "A" sounds as in *Hop* rather than *Hope*, or as in *(G)lad* rather than *Led*. The modern descendants like Gujarati, use a flipped sign for this: ◼. I had to use Gujarati fonts to show you this.

Dead	ठ३
Dad	ठ३
Fed	ईઙ
Fad	ईઙ
Hope	હોપ
Hop	હોપ

This sign is not used in Sanskrit, because before today no one has had the temerity to write English words in the script meant for Sanskrit!

It is never adequate to show you in writing how to pronounce a particular sound. Sometimes we have no choice. But you do have a choice. Probably there are people around you, among your family, friends, etc. who can show you the correct pronunciation, once and for all. I am just trying to help you follow what they might say.

An audio or a video tape is not the answer. Learning the mother tongue, or the mother of mother tongues is a family affair, and there should be no wedge to separate one from the family. Unlike in German, or in French, one does not have to learn how to pronounce each and every one of innumerable words. In case of Devanagari, you have to know the pronunciation only once.

The More the Merrier!

When we looked at the letters for Bh, Ph, Gh sounds, we did not talk about the Ch sound. Of course you are familiar with Chair, Child, Chore, etc. However, there is a minor difference. The two parts of Ch, that is, "C" and "h" are not related to each other.

There is no real "C" sound, unlike the "B" or "P" sound. Yes, there are two sounds conveyed by "C", viz., "K" sound, as in Cat, Cut, Catch, etc., and the "S" sound, as in Nice, Cycle, Choice, etc., but no "C" sound as such. Therefore, "CH" by itself is a unique sound.

What's the point of this whole story? Well, like Bh, and Dh, we also have a CHh sound. Again, you say the CH and H together, as in "Ah..ch.hoo!" or in "Ch.hu...ch.hu" train. The letter for that is छ.

See: लांछन   A blemish

        छत्र   A head shield

        छत्री, छाता   An umbrella (in Hindi)

Aspiring to Learn:

As your list of equivalents will show you, there are many letters in Devanagari, that stand for two letters in English, e.g. ध, फ, घ, ख, भ, etc., which stand for Dh, Ph, Gh, Kh, and Bh respectively.

Westerners have no problem with the first five, but the last one throws them off. In these letters, "h" is pronounced simultaneously with the preceding letter, and not sequentially. We say "Philosophy", and not "Pahilosopahy".

Similarly, "Bh" is not pronounced as "Bah". As in the first four letters, combining "h" with another sound, produces an entirely new sound. The original two sounds are not discernible anymore.

Write the following words containing the letters with an "h" sound (called "Aspirates", because you have to breathe in before you can say them out loud):

Jazz	→	जाझ
Rough	→	रफ
Them	→	धेम
Ghost	→	घोस्ट
Paksh (wing, sides in a dispute)	→	पक्ष
Bharat	→	भरत

Bh<u>a</u>rat	→	भारत. India's official name, after a king called भरत.
Ayatolla Khoummani	→	आयातोल्ला खोमेनी
George Bush	→	ज्योर्ज बुश
Washington	→	वोशिंग्टन

The Third Half:

Just to review quickly the various ways to create conjoined consonants. As you may recall, all English letters are half, or devoid of a vowel. The Devanagari ones already have the vowel अ included in them. You also remember that some letters like त, न, म, ग, have a दंड or "a stick" built in them, while others like ट, ड, ठ, do not.

What are the ways you can get a conjoined consonant,

    1.   From a letter with a दंड? → Remove the दंड, and then join it to the next letter, लास्ट

    2.   If there is no दंड? → Literally join it to the next letter, एक्टर

You did remember these two ways of getting a half letter. You also know one more, although you may not remember it as such. Let me refresh your memory.

3.   What about half म and न ?   →   Put a dot on the preceding letter. That's the third way, पंप, बंट

4.   Can that also be done for any other letters?   →   Yes, with ञ, ण, ङ

5.   Which letters are practically never written out?   →   ञ and ङ

There is yet another and easier way to obtain a half letter. This is not an extra burden, unless you are working hard to commit all this to memory. This is one more tool to help you. The best part is, it works with any kind of letter, be it nasal, with a दंड, or without one. Ready?

I am sure you still remember the "inverted check mark" ◣ sign that we put on top of a letter, मेरी (Mary, Marry, Merry). A similar sign at the bottom of any consonant ◤ will make that consonant half. Let us go back to Smita and Bhaskar.

How do we write these?

   Smita   →   स्मिता

   Bhaskar   →   भास्कर

   Sent   →   सेंट

   Sant   (A saint. How similar!)   →   संत

Can you write "Sant" in three ways?   →   १. संत
                                     २. सन्त
                                       ३. सन्त

Using the new way we just learned, write

Smita	→	स्मिता
Bhaskar	→	भास्कर
Sent	→	सेन्ट
Fantastic	→	फेन्टास्टीक

☞ Do not confuse ◤ with ◣ Look at these carefully:

भास्कर   भासूकर (a meaningless word)

Please note that while we treat conjoined consonants as one letter, the half letter obtained in the newly learnt manner is treated as an independent entity. Compare the following:

स्मिता   स्मिता

This ◤ way of making a half letter is used extremely commonly. You will see many many examples of it as we go along.

A Curse In Disguise !

Just one last item before we conclude. It won't be fair to leave you unattended in the forest of conjoined consonants, especially when any half letter is joined to र.

Let us get "RI" or ऋ out of the way. It is a vowel, and is used either as such, or as ◼ as in पार्ट, or as ◼ as in कृष्ण.

रु is same as रु

रू   रू

ऋ   RI, there is no ◼ी.

For reasons beyond the scope of the present work, when any half letter is joined to र, the र disappears, and a tent like sign is put at the bottom: ◼, of the supposedly half letter, which looks like anything but half !

Tram	ट्राम
Drama	ड्रामा

When the half letter has a दंड, only half the tent sign ◼ appears in the angle between the दंड and the main body of the letter:

Progress		प्रोग्रेस
Cross		क्रोस (क्रोस)
Kendra	(Center)	केंद्र, केन्द्र
Shrim<u>a</u>n	(Mr.)	श्रीमान्
		(श्रीमान्, श्रीमान्)

Thank you for your patience, although I have been doing all the work. We must enjoy the journey also, rather than asking every few minutes "Are we there yet?" We have been talking about vowels, their symbols, consonants - half and full, numerals, and punctuation marks, etc.

Now you are ready to meet formally, the Devanagari alphabet itself. There is nothing for you to do. Just sit back and enjoy.

ENGLISH EQUIVALENTS OF

DEVANAGARI VOWELS AND CONSONANTS

Consonants:

क   ख   ग   घ   ङ   (No word begins with ङ)
k   kh   g   gh   ng

च   छ   ज   झ   ञ   (No word begins with ञ)
ch   chh   j   jh/z yn

ट   ठ   ड   ढ   ण   (No word begins with ण)
t   th   d   dh   n

(As you know, the pronunciation of the letters in this row, and in the next one below this, are not identical)

त   थ   द   ध   न
t   th   d   th   n

प   फ   ब   भ   म
p   ph/f b   bh   m

य   र   ल   व
y   r   l   v / w

श   ष   स
s   sh   sh   (The middle one is used less frequently)

ह   ळ   (No word begins with ळ)
h   r / l

क्ष   ज्ञ
ksh   gnya   (Actually, these two are special conjoined consonants)

Vowels and Their Symbols:

अ	आ	अि	ई	उ	ऊ			ऋ		
■	■ा	ि■	■ी	■ु	■ू			ᴄ	■	■
A	Aa	I	EE	U	OO			Ri	Part	Krishna

ए	ऐ	ओ	औ	अं	अः
■	■	■ो	■ौ	■	■ः
E	Ai	O	Au	Um	Ah

Special Symbols:

■	Indicates a half letter	सन्त, फ्लीन्ट
■	As in Tram, Drama	ट्राम, ड्रामा
⅃	As in Progress, Creation	प्रोग्रेस, क्रीएशन

Alphabetical Order:

Devanagari alphabet is read from left to right, and from top to bottom. It goes from क to ज्ञ. First of all, note that there are 12 vowels, and 36 consonants. Also note that,

क्ष is क्श, or क्श

and ज्ञ is ग्न or ग्न्य

Therefore, in a dictionary, क्ष will appear under क, and ज्ञ will appear under ग.

It is also important to note that the vowel ऋ follows ऊ, and precedes ए.

There are many Sanskrit into English dictionaries available. Now you should be able to take advantage of them.

The alphabetical order is this:

Vowels
Consonants

Arrange the following in alphabetical order:

बोम्बे   → अमेरिका

अमेरिका   बोम्बे

लंडन   लंडन

Under each consonant, just like in any English dictionary, the words will be listed according to their second and subsequent letters.

Arrange the following in alphabetical order:

कार   → कम्पाला (युगान्डा)

कोमेडीअन   काउ Vowel first

क्रोस   कार Then consonant

काउ   कोमेडीअन

कम्पाला (युगान्डा)   क्रोस Half letter last

Don't let the following bother you. You may never need this. Each letter will be listed in the order of its accompanying vowel. That is, क, का, कि, की, ...कौ ।

कं, कः are applied to each of these. So, the order will be क, कं, कः, through कौ, कौं, कौः. This will then be followed by the half letter: क्ट, क्प, क्र (क्र), etc., again in the alphabetical order of the complete letter.

Everything In Its Proper Place:

Below, I have grouped the first 25 consonants in a 5x5 box. There is a very impressive order in that arrangement.

Say each row (horizontal) out loud, one after the other, and note that all five letters in any row are pronounced by keeping the tongue and lips, etc. in one particular way.

Where are क....ङ said from? ➔ The throat. All the way back. These are *Gutturals*.

च...ञ ➔ From the soft palate, at the back of the roof of the mouth. These are *Palatals*.

ट...ण ➔ From the hard palate, retroflexing the tongue.

त...न ➔ These are *Dentals*. Your tongue has to touch the back of your teeth.

प...म ➔ These are *Labials*. Note your lips getting into the action.

Now, if you still have difficulty in pronouncing a letter, you can try to pronounce it in the same way in which all the other letters from the same row are pronounced.

All this is very interesting. Mind you, we are dealing with a language that is 5-10,000 years old. What a scientific and orderly arrangement!

The extreme right hand column (vertical) shows all five nasal sounds, ङ, ञ, ण, न, म. Note that each group (row) has its own nasal sound.

Which of these nasal letters are written and used as whole letters?

→ न, म, ण.

When used as half letters, all five can be replaced or represented by a dot over the previous letter. The pronunciation of the dot is automatically governed by the letter that follows.

Once again, let me demonstrate this to you. I have given below a few words using a dot. The first letter is ब in all of them, while the letter after the dot is different. Read these out loud, and notice how the sound represented by the dot varies.

Bunk	बंक	बङ्क
Bunch	बंच	बञ्च
Bunt	बंट	बण्ट
Bundh	बंध	बन्ध
Bump	बंप	बम्प

In the above, the letter after the dot is in order, from the क, च, ट, त, प group respectively. You do not have to do anything in this.

☞ The pronunciation of the sound represented by the dot is *automatically* decided by the letter just after it. No conscious effort is required.

There is more to this order that will interest you. There are many things we do in

English without quite knowing why we do them. For example, look at the words *Education*, and *Punctual*.

Write in Devanagari:

Education   → एज्युकेशन

Punctual   → पंक्च्युअल

What has happened?   → D has become J in एज्युकेशन and T has become CH in पंक्च्युअल. Please do not say ""Di", "Je", "Ti", and "Si-Ech". Just say the sounds.

Now, this is in English, not in Sanskrit. We don't even bother to think about such things in English. There is a good reason for this: It is all done automatically. We don't have to think about it.

☞   Remember that well. *We don't have to think about it. We don't have to memorize it.* Ignorance of this simple fact has compelled innumerable students of Sanskrit to engage in memorizing tens and hundreds of "rules" for such changes. Spare yourself the trouble.

Look at the Devanagari alphabet we just saw. Notice how close ड and ज are, and how close ट and च are.

Whenever two consonants are joined together, or when two vowels occur next to each other, some changes in pronunciation automatically take place. They are interesting to look at. We will cross that bridge when we come to it.

Cut That Out !

Before we leave the alphabet, let me show you one last symbol. It is actually a punctuation mark, which is used extremely commonly in Sanskrit.

It is like an apostrophe mark — a sign of deletion— e.g., Boy's, It's, You're, I'm, etc. It looks like the English letter "S".

Which Devanagari letter looks like "S"?

➜ ड

So, how would we write this new symbol ?

➜ Like this: ऽ

It is called अवग्रह चिह्न (ह + न). You don't have to remember that, but it is good to know the signs by their names.

What's the difference between ड and the new sign ऽ?

➜ Punctuation marks do not have a line at the top.

ऽ is generally used to indicate a missing अ. For example:

कालः अपि

कालो अपि

कालोऽपि

We will see many examples of that later. For now, let me just show you how it compares with similar Devanagari letters:

ड ऽ इ

Note that it has no line at the top. Also compare it with ड quite well to see that it doesn't quite extend to the baseline, nor does it have a miniscule vertical line suspending it from the top.

How do we pronounce it? Well, we don't! It is a punctuation mark, not a vowel symbol. It is not a letter of the alphabet. Then why don't we cut it out? Because, if we do cut something out, we'll have to put that sign there. And that's why I had to show it to you !

❖ ❖ ❖

You have just completed
learning all the consonants, vowels, punctuation marks,
and mathematical symbols in the Devanagari script.

Believe it or not,
maybe with a little more practice,
but you are, and you should be able to
read and write anything and everything that is written
in the Devanagari script,
be it in Hindi, Marathi, or in Sanskrit,
with confidence, and without being intimidated by it.

Mind well,
that such a statement can never be made for
the English language.
My most sincere compliments to you!

BOOKS BY BHARAT S. SHAH, M.D.

Sanskrit: An Appreciation without Apprehension
(Includes *A Crash Course to Learn the Devanagari Script*
Second edition. Our bestseller on the internet) $24

An Introduction to Jainism
(Second edition. Our bestseller on the internet) $18
(First edition, while the supplies last) $15

Programmed Text to Learn Gujarati (Second edition) $20

A Crash Course to Learn the Gujarati Script $3

A Crash Course to Learn the Devanagari Script
Used for Sanskrit, Hindi, and Marathi languages
(First edition, while supplies last, see below)   *$3*

English for the Grandma (In Gujarati) $15

NEW ARRIVALS 2010-13

Dawn at Midnight *(A documentary novel on awaiting*
liver transplant) $12
Dawn at Midnight (**Kindle E-book**) $7

Sameepe (A documentary popular novel,
the original version of "Dawn at Midnight," in Gujarati.
Not available on Internet. Please Email the author) $10

My Life with Panic Disorder (A documentary novel) $10
My Life with Panic Disorder (Kindle E-book) $6

Questions Answers Exclamations:
From the Garage of a Clinical Researcher
(Author's ideas for medical research being bequeathed
to the future generation. $15

Capitalism, colonization of America, and
The Mating Habits of the Praying Mantis
On how we managed to get into the financial morass,
and became our own colony. $8
Kindle E-book $5

A Crash Course to Learn the Devanagari Script
Used for Sanskrit, Hindi, and Marathi languages
(Second expanded edition 2013)   *$6*

All these books are in English, unless noted otherwise. They are available from amazon.com. Their detailed descriptions, cover images, sample pages, readers' reviews, comments, and shipping information, are available on website of amazon.

Made in the USA
Middletown, DE
10 February 2020

84453296R00038